JOYCE
IMAGES

Introduction by Anthony Burgess

JOYCE IMAGES

Conceived and Designed by Bob Cato

Edited by Greg Vitiello

W.W. NORTON & COMPANY
New York   London

Copyright © 1994 by Bob Cato
© Introduction 1994 by Anthony Burgess
First Edition

The text of this book is composed in Cartier
with the display in hand lettering and script.
Composition by C.T. Photogenic Graphics, Inc. and COMP24.
Manufacturing by Arnoldo Mondadori Editore, Verona, Italy.
Book design by Bob Cato.

Tom Stoppard's *Travesties*, published in the U.K. by Faber & Faber Ltd.;
published in the U.S. by Grove Atlantic Inc.
Reprinted with permission.

Library of Congress Cataloging-in-Publication Data

Cato, Bob.
Joyce images / concept and design, Bob Cato;
editor, Greg Vitiello; introduction by Anthony Burgess
p. cm.

1. Joyce, James, 1882–1941—Pictorial Works. 2. Novelists,
Irish—20th century—Biography—Pictorial works.
I. Vitiello, Greg. II. Title.
PR6019.09Z526375   1994
823′.912—dc20
[B]   93–45332
CIP
ISBN 0-393-03638-3

Printed in Italy

W.W. Norton & Company, Inc., 500 Fifth Avenue, New York, N.Y. 10110
W.W. Norton & Company, Ltd., 10 Coptic Street, London WC1A 1PU

1 2 3 4 5 6 7 8 9 0

CONCEIVED AND DESIGNED BY: *Bob Cato*
EDITED BY: *Greg Vitiello*
EDITORIAL ASSOCIATES: *Kate Jennings & Jane Kagan Vitiello*

TITLE PAGE: *Joyce sent this photograph of himself to Paul and Lucie Léon in 1935.*

ACKNOWLEDGMENTS

In compiling this book, we have received much help and counsel. We are grateful to many individuals and institutions for providing images for our use. We are especially grateful to Stephen and Solange Joyce, who gave us their insights, support, hospitality—and yes, their friendship. Through our contact with them, we learned much about Stephen's grandparents, James and Nora Joyce. They also directed us to others who made important contributions to this book—particularly Stephen's niece Judy Fleischman, the artist Louis LeBrocquy, and Jacques Davidson, the son of sculptor Jo Davidson. We thank them all.

We received valuable advice from Jean-Yves Mallet, Martha Fehsenfeld, Phillip Lyman of the James Joyce Society, and Robert Spoo, editor of the *James Joyce Quarterly*. We wish to thank Fritz Senn, Ruth Frehner, and Ursula Zeller of the Zurich James Joyce Foundation, who supplied us with images and useful advice; Peter C. Jones of the Breitenbach Trust and Susan Arthur of the Houk Friedman Gallery of New York, who made available to us the extraordinary set of photographs by Josef Breitenbach; Jay Jennings and Jessica Green, who graciously allowed us to use their portrait of Joyce, which appears on the cover of this book; and Horst Tappe, who photographed Ezra Pound's visit to Joyce's gravesite in Zurich.

In Ireland, we were fortunate to have the assistance of Robert Nicholson, director of the James Joyce Museum; Ken Monaghan; Patrick Prendergast; Vivien Igoe; and Louis O'Byrne of the Central Bank of Ireland, who granted us use of the newly issued ten-pound note that bears Joyce's image.

Many of the images in this book were supplied to us by the curator, Robert Bertholf, and Michael Basinski of the Poetry/Rare Books Collection, State University of New York at Buffalo; our special thanks to them. Others who supplied images, and whom we thank, include the curator, Vincent Giroud, and Rick Hart of the Beinecke Rare Book & Manuscript Library at Yale University; Lori Curtis, McFarlin Library, University of Tulsa; Elizabeth Neubauer, Harry Ransom Humanities Research Center, University of Texas at Austin; Peggy Roche of the Morris Library, Southern Illinois University at Carbondale; H. Thomas Hickerson, Division of Rare and Manuscript Collections, Carl A. Kroch Library, Cornell University; Margaret Sherry and Alice Clark, Department of Rare Books and Special Collections, Princeton University Libraries; Constance Kimmerle, Rosenbach Museum & Library; and Russell Maylone, Special Collections, Northwestern University Library.

Others who provided images, and who merit our thanks, include Helaine Pardo of Commerce Graphics for the several photographs by Berenice Abbott; Andrew Hoyem, publisher of Arion Press; Suzanne Goldstein of Photo Researchers, Inc.; the *New York Review of Books*; and Archive Photos. We especially thank Adelaide Jones and Swissair for providing transportation for our research in Europe.

We were fortunate to work with Anthony Burgess, a great and abiding champion of Joyce's writings, who completed his wise and lucid introduction just three months before his death in November 1993. Literature is poorer for his loss.

We thank Bob Cato's mother, Ysabel Cristofalina Soto, who read to him from *Ulysses* when he was just eight years old and who gave him a 1926 edition of the book which he still has.

And we particularly thank Mary Cunnane, who had the foresight to commission this book and the sage advice and support that helped bring it to fruition.●

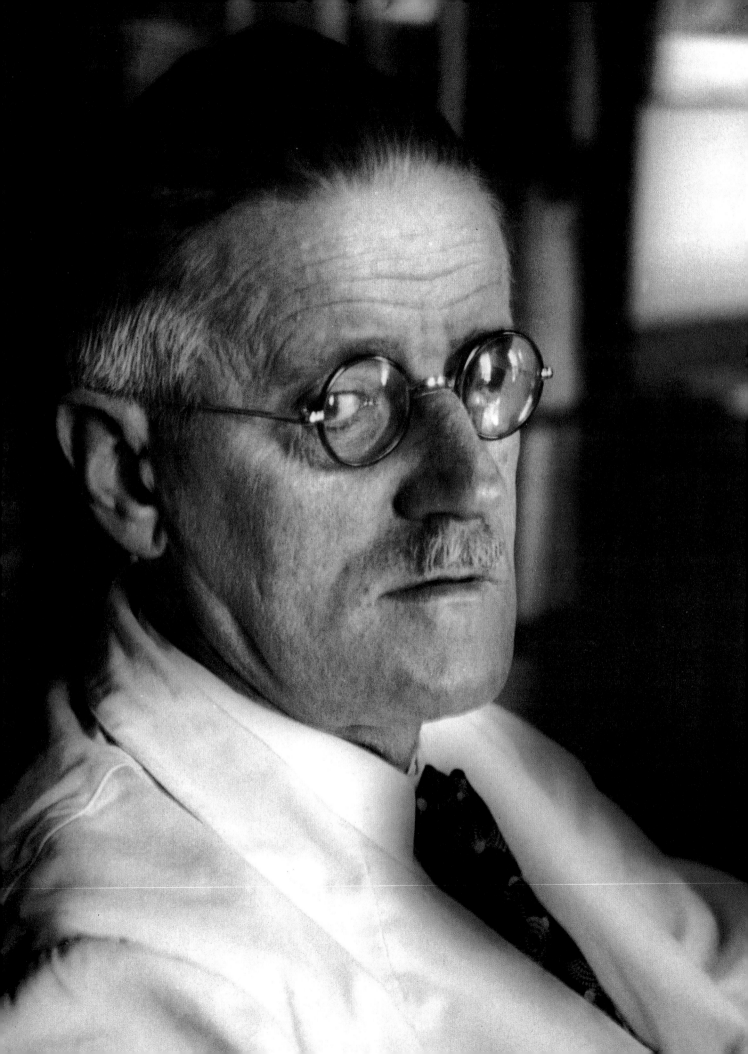

Anthony Burgess

JAMES JOYCE was the most paradoxical of writers. He was banned as an obscene subverter of morality while in fact possessing an unshakable faith in marital fidelity and family stability. He was almost as blind as his predecessors in the epic line, Homer and Milton, and yet no writer has appealed more to professional visualizers—whether painters, photographers, or filmmakers. In his later work, he distorted and rarefied language to the limit, but no writer more celebrated the banalities and joys of ordinary life. A Dubliner whose books were written in exile, he had no other subject than the lives of Dubliners. In *Ulysses*, the Dublin of June 16, 1904, is set before us, unfantasized, verifiable in most of its details from maps and directories. The novel begins in the Martello Tower on the Dublin coast at Sandymount, a locale which, before it was turned into a Joyce museum, made the visitor feel that he had eerily entered the book itself and was likely to get in the way of the action. *Ulysses*, which glorifies Dublin by turning it into an eternal city of the mind, had modified it in sober, or drunken, fact. Entering Dublin, one enters *Ulysses* and even *Finnegans Wake*; one enters Joyce's imagination.

Joyce was so little of a visual writer that he created characters one can hardly see, though one can hear them vividly enough. None of his main characters are described: they are voices, though not disembodied ones. Leopold and Molly Bloom are, God knows, fleshy enough: Bloom can be weighed and measured, but he discloses no image in any mirror. Perhaps this lack of visibility has impelled the visual recorders to fill up an apparent emptiness. As for the invisible city of Dublin, we have only to visit it to make it visible: never before or after in literary history have the reality and its representation been so firmly fused into a symbiosis.

This relationship is reinforced by the fact that Joyce, alone among major novelists, invented very little outside the verbal sphere. His language dances or goes mad or is frighteningly accurate in a way hardly known before, but the language serves its subject matter and not itself. Joyce's first prose work, the

James Joyce, Paris, 1937, photographed by Josef Breitenbach.
This sequence of photographs on pages 6-15 appears for the
first time in any publication, courtesy of the Breitenbach Trust
and Houk Friedman Gallery, New York.

volume of short stories called, with disarming literalness, *Dubliners*, established a cast list of the city's lower middle-class boozers, layabouts, dreamers, failures, liars, which would be called upon in *Ulysses*. All are based on real-life contemporaries of Joyce. This was an aspect of *Dubliners* that hindered its publication. The secondary hero of *Ulysses*, Telemachus to Bloom's Odysseus, is Stephen Dedalus, Joyce himself at the age of 22. Behind the image of the young, unwashed, half-starved poet is the full-length study of *A Portrait of the Artist as a Young Man*—a very ironical title when one considers that the book is a masterly celebration of dim sight. Here is Stephen from babyhood to early maturity, with the real Joyce family present though faintly seen—except for the father, the witty drunken reprobate whom his children feared and hated but James alone loved.

A Portrait appalled some of its early readers with its realism. Yet the exact notation of real life is in the service of a symbolism that makes the book a landmark in literary modernism. The soul of the poet is in danger of turning into a fish when it aspires to be a bird. On the very first page the infant Stephen wets the bed. Bogs and mud and waterholes try to suck him down, but he succeeds at last in taking to the air in free flight, a bird singing of liberation. The name Stephen Dedalus, which must be considered implausible, is crammed with symbolism. Stephen was the first martyr, and his namesake must be ready for the suffering attendant on a devotion to art. Daedalus (that digraph would have been going too far in a realistic narrative) was the fabulous artificer in the service of King Minos, who built the wooden cow in which Queen Pasiphae was impregnated, laid out the labyrinth that imprisoned her half-divine man-bull offspring, the Minotaur, and finally, with his son Icarus, dared the heavens with artificial wings. In *A Portrait*, Stephen invokes Daedalus as a father and himself becomes Icarus. He is ready to fly but recognizes that, as in the legend, he may fly too near the sun, find the wax of his wings melting, fall into the ocean. A winged creature falling from heaven suggests Lucifer. Stephen is prepared to take on that part too; he uses Lucifer's words *"Non serviam"*—I will not serve.

A Portrait, commenced and abandoned in Dublin, was finally a fine fruit of Joyce's exile in Trieste. He saw himself as proud and solitary, but he did not leave Ireland as a lone voyager. On June 16, 1904, he declared love for Nora Barnacle, a girl from Galway who was working as a chambermaid in Finn's Hotel, Dublin. She agreed to share her life with him. Joyce abandoned the Church of Rome and would not have marriage nor, when the time came for children, baptism. Eventually, as a photograph shows us, Joyce and Nora married in 1931 in London in a secular ceremony "for testamentary reasons," but the earlier, tempestuous phase of their lives was lived in what the Church called sin. Their two children, Giorgio and Lucia, were "bastards." But Joyce's devotion to his family was absolute; the day of his declaration of love was to become the day of *Ulysses*, or Bloomsday. In the autumn of the year, penniless but equipped with a degree from University College, Dublin, he left for the Continent.

His fellow students at UCD had wanted him to become a citizen of an Ireland closing in on itself, speaking Erse and not English, dourly Catholic, morally pure. But Joyce, surrounded by obscurantist priests and peasant-booted louts in heavy homespun, desired the bigger world. He saw free thought and moral emancipation personified in Henrik Ibsen, whose Dano-Norwegian he mastered sufficiently to write an adulatory letter to the great man. He had learned French, Italian, German, but not Erse. He was to become the ideal European polyglot. As a teacher of English he was employed by the Berlitz school in Trieste, in the great port of the Austro-Hungarian Empire. Here, off-duty, he lived the drunken convivial life that kept him poor, and furthered his ambitions as a writer. *Ulysses* was begun in Trieste. Its hero is a very modern man, a Jewish advertising canvasser. Dubliners still wonder how Joyce could create so improbable a fiction: Jews, they insist, were not to be seen in the Ireland of 1904. True, they were not prominent, they had not risen to dominate town councils, but they were there. Joyce's Jew, however, seems to be more a product of Trieste where Jews abounded. He seems particularly based on one of Joyce's pupils, Ettore Schmitz, who, as Italo Svevo, achieved belated fame as a novelist. It was Joyce who fostered his talent and was to provide the English title—*As a Man Grows Older*—for his masterpiece *La Senilitá*.

Joyce had had, as an idea for a short story for *Dubliners*, a parody of the *Odyssey* expressed as a single brief day in Dublin, but the notion grew. The common man of the twentieth century, typically a Jew, specialist in oppression, alienation, and the citizenship of exile, should be exalted into an Odysseus or Ulysses, albeit comically. His Penelope should be a Hispano-Irish wife from Gibraltar, with a good deal of Nora Barnacle in her (her final monstrous monologue is based on Nora's epistolary style). What should be the plot? Odysseus, after the siege of Troy, tries to get back to Ithaca, his island kingdom, where his dear son Telemachus is holding the fort against the insolent suitors who seek the hand, and wealth, of the supposed widow Penelope. His journey is slowed, occasionally near-aborted, by a number of grotesque adventures. In Joyce's parody, these are given a modern, usually symbolic form. The one-eyed Cyclops becomes the chauvinistic, xenophobic citizen, who hurls a biscuit tin at Bloom, but the Lestrygonians are not cannibals, merely dirty eaters, and the perilous path between Scylla and Charybdis is merely an academic discussion, led by Stephen, that veers between the rock of Aristotle and the whirlpool of Plato. There are highly superficial parallels but also highly satisfying ones. Bloom comes through his brutal adventures more or less unscathed. He even finds a surrogate son in Stephen, whom he lures back to Ithaca. Stephen will not stay the night there, but we have a feeling that the real story will begin on June 17, 1904.

Begun in Trieste, *Ulysses* was continued in Zurich (where Joyce moved in 1915, some months after the First World War erupted and he found himself a British subject on enemy soil). Here the chapter celebrating the Sirens, written in the form of a fugue, beginning with a disjunct catalogue of verbal themes like the bones of the Sirens' victims, was seized by the Swiss authorities as a suspected communication in code to one or another of the belligerents in the Great War. Joyce had promised to be neutral, British though he was.

In Zurich Joyce's luck with women, which had begun with his finding Nora, continued. He was supported by Edith McCormick, a fabulously wealthy American lady. At the same time Joyce was discovered by Ezra Pound, always in the van of the friends of new art, and this led to his further discovery by Miss Harriet Shaw Weaver, a Quaker Englishwoman who owned *The Egoist*, in which *A Portrait* was serialized. She became Joyce's lifelong financial support. She enabled him to work at the uncommercial venture of *Finnegans Wake*; she inadvertently encouraged a certain dissoluteness and was not amused by it. Her loyalty was remarkable; she was the last of the great patrons.

Joyce's final exilic move was to Paris, where, in a milieu very favorable to literary experiment, he completed *Ulysses*. It is Joyce's Paris life, the years of his fame, that has drawn the photographers. The conviviality continued, though now with a literary set that included such other exiles as Ernest Hemingway, Pound, and Ford Madox Ford. Moneyed men like the lawyer John Quinn came in from New York, ready to buy manuscripts. As *Ulysses* drew to its close and was partly serialized in the *The Little Review* and *The Egoist*, its alleged obscenity caused trouble: no Anglophone publisher or printer seemed likely to touch it. In the usual paradox, those who found it obscene also found it unintelligible. The Homeric parallels suggested narrative techniques appropriate to the subject

matter but not always clear in intention to the uninstructed reader, meaning nearly everyone. The obstacles against commercial publication were immense.

Again, Joyce was lucky with a woman. This was a young American spinster, Miss Sylvia Beach, who, on November 17, 1919, founded the bookshop on the Left Bank known as Shakespeare and Company. Her father had served in Paris at the Presbyterian ministry to Americans and had passed his love of France on to his daughter. In the 1914–18 war she served her adopted country in the *Volontaires Agricoles*, with bobbed hair and khaki culottes, but Paris called her back from the cabbage patches. There she met Adrienne Monnier, who kept a bookshop, La Maison des Amis des Livres, on the rue de l'Odéon, which was to become the second and final home of Shakespeare and Company. They became friends and probably more. It was the extracurricular activities of Adrienne Monnier's *librairie* that inspired Sylvia to set up her own center of expatriate culture. *Chez* Adrienne she heard André Gide read, also Schlumberger, Fargue, Larbaud. Soon her bookshop encouraged visits from expatriate writers passing through or, indeed, staying. Joyce was one.

Her courageous act in proposing that she be the publisher of *Ulysses*, when no regular entrepreneur in London or New York would take on the task, has earned her a high place among the heroines who helped Joyce. She arranged for the printing to be done in Dijon, then the capital of the French printing world, and Maurice Darantiere, knowing no English and unaware of the dynamite he was handling, achieved a great feat in bringing out the 1922 edition of *Ulysses*. Though inevitably crammed with errors (but not more than in later, Anglophone printings), it was a great gift for Joyce's fortieth birthday (February 2) and a revelation or a bomb to the rest of the world.

The book, as we know, was banned in the United States until December 1933, when Judge John M. Woolsey of the U.S. District Court of New York wisely declared that there was something emetic about *Ulysses* but nothing at all obscene. Until then, Joyce was less upset about the allegations of dirt than about the loss of sales and the piracy of an unscrupulous American publisher. His high place in art offered small consolation for his failure to make money from his work.

Meanwhile, his sight was deteriorating; he required a great many painful eye operations that seemed to do little good. The composition of his next and final work, the prospect of which pleased very few, had to be pursued on a blackboard in large letters. This was to be called *Finnegans Wake*; in the 1930s, when it appeared in periodical pamphlet selections, it was called *Work in Progress*. Joyce liked his mysteries, and he thought that the too early disclosure of his title would give too easy a clue to his subject matter. This book is, in fact, about death and resurrection, and the Irish god Finn figures large. The lack of an apostrophe points to multiple meanings: the wake of dead Finnegan, the waking of all the Finnegans, an end (fin) and a resumption (egan or again). It is a vast punning book. It is the record of a night's dreaming as *Ulysses* is one of a day's crammed activity. It was not meant to be easy reading. Nora wondered

why he did not write a nice book for nice people to enjoy. The answer probably was that *Finnegans Wake* had to be written, and that Joyce had been chosen by the cruel gods of literature to write it.

He sometimes despaired of being able to finish it, and he was so superstitious that he thought James Stephens ought to take on the task. Stephens was the leprechaunish poet who, like Joyce, was born on February 2, 1882; he contained in his name both Joyce's baptismal bestowal and that of young Dedalus. This was enough. But the task was left to its initiator.

As a diversion, Joyce soothed himself by consulting the needs of the tenor John Sullivan, whose voice fulfilled all the dead aspirations of Joyce's own. For Joyce, as a young man, had had a fine musical talent, a magnificent tessitura; he had, however, a certain vocal thinness suitable for folk songs and drawing-room ballads but not for Rossini's *Guillaume Tell*. This was the opera in which, thanks to Joyce's persistence, Sullivan was eventually able to please Paris.

Joyce's triumph, however, was short-lived, for he was soon preoccupied with the plight of his daughter, Lucia. She had grown in her Paris years into winsome girlhood, chic, a fine dancer, her beauty marred or enhanced by a slight strabismus—or squint. She was developing, invisibly to the Joyces but not to others, an incurable schizophrenia. What the world called madness Joyce thought of as a talent not unlike his own, a capacity to push beyond common sense and logic to a world of new truths. The great psychiatrist Jung contrasted Lucia's condition and Joyce's genius: Joyce was diving, Lucia was sinking. She and Joyce's deteriorating eyesight, added to the immense labor of *Finnegans Wake*, made the late 1930s a time of misery. But Harriet Shaw Weaver was there to comfort, cajole, and encourage.

Joyce's final book appeared in the spring of 1939. It baffled most of its reviewers. The war was coming, and *Finnegans Wake* looked like an image of universal breakdown. Proust's masterpiece, *Remembrance of Things Past*, had been blamed for the decay of France, a ripely rotten fruit for the invader's picking, whereas it had merely shown, with the clarity of genius, the symptoms of breakdown. Joyce, through a kind of dream code, was presenting a formula for the reestablishing of cosmos out of chaos. This seemed to be the end of his literary career, though he was only in his late fifties and he talked vaguely of writing something simple. War came, the Nazis entered Paris. Joyce and his family had to escape to Zurich, that refuge of an earlier war, though the Swiss authorities at first made difficulties. Joyce had created a Jew, ergo he was himself a Jew, and the Jewish quota of refugeeship was full. *"Enfin e'est le bouquet,"* Joyce gasped.

In Zurich in 1941, he died after an operation for a ruptured stomach ulcer. In Zurich he is buried, his grave surmounted by a sculpture by Milton Hebald, one of many images by which he is remembered. And of course, the work is still there, is in fact there more than ever, and it continues to modify the lives of those who know it. ●

He left Zurich after the war, went to Paris,
stayed twenty years, and turned up here again in December 1940.
Another war...But he was a sick man then, perforated ulcer, and in January he was dead...
buried one cold snowy day in the Fluntern Cemetery up the hill.

I dreamed about him, dreamed I had him in the witness box, a masterly cross-examination,
case practically won, admitted it all, the whole thing, the trousers, everything, and I flung at
him—"And what did you do in the Great War?" "I wrote Ulysses," he said. "What did
you do?"

Bloody nerve.

Henry Carr, a character in TOM STOPPARD'S
Travesties, End of Act I

Joyce at about age 30.

Two images of Joyce at age 6½, including one with his parents,
John and Mary Jane, and his maternal grandfather, John Murray.

Joyce with fellow students and faculty at Clongowes Wood School, which he attended from 1888 to 1891. Upon his arrival there, he said his age was "Half past six," which became his school nickname.

When asked what he thought while family friend C. F. Curran photographed him in 1904, Joyce said, "I wondered would he lend me five shillings."

This photo ran in the New York Post Library Review in 1923 with the caption: "Author of the much-discussed Ulysses when an undergraduate in Dublin —From an unpublished photograph."

On his first trip to Paris in 1902, Joyce sent his friend John Byrne a postcard with a photo of him in a long coat and a poem headed "Second Part—opening which tells of the journeyings of the soul."

Second Part — Opening which tells of the
journeyings of the Soul.

—

All day I hear the noise of waters
    Making moan,
Sad as the sea-bird is when going
    Forth alone
4: hears the winds cry to the waters'
    Monotone.

⌒

The grey winds, the cold winds are blowing
    Where I go;
I hear the noise of many waters
    Far below,
All day, all night I hear them flowing
    To and fro.

Hotel Corneille
5 Rue Corneille, Paris

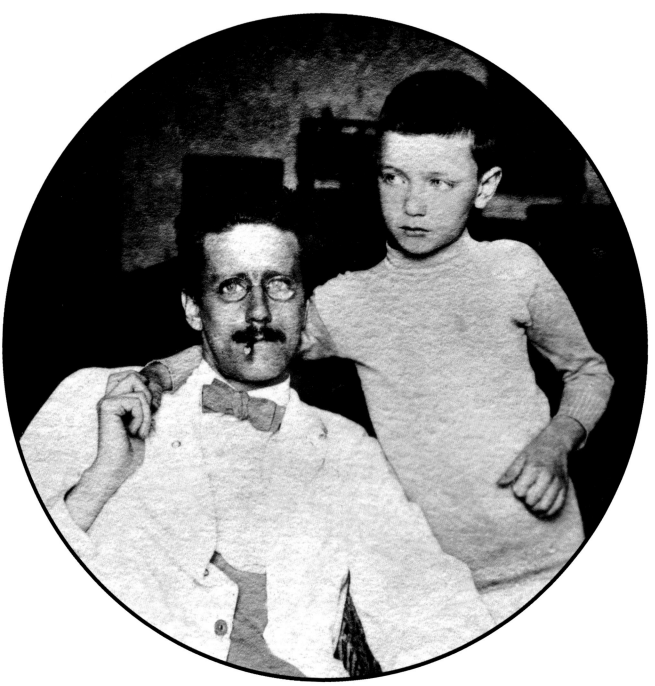

Joyce with Giorgio in Trieste, 1914.

Nora Barnacle Joyce, with Giorgio, 13, and Lucia, 11, in Zurich, 1918.

Nora in Zurich in about 1920.

*"…on June 10, 1904, Joyce was walking down Nassau Street [in Dublin] when he caught
sight of a tall, good-looking young woman, auburn-haired, walking with a proud stride. When he
spoke to her she answered pertly enough to allow the conversation to continue….
Her name was a little comic, Nora Barnacle…."*
—Richard Ellmann, James Joyce

Wyndham Lewis. 1921.

Wyndham Lewis's drawing of Joyce, 1921. A year earlier, after meeting Joyce in Paris, Lewis wrote of his fellow author: "I found an oddity, in patent-leather shoes, large powerful spectacles, and a small gingerbread beard; speaking half in voluble Italian to a scowling schoolboy; playing the Irishman a little overmuch perhaps, but in amusingly mannered technique."

Joyce in Trieste, about 1919.

Joyce in Trieste, 1915. Ottocaro Weiss, a friend who took the photograph, was impressed by Joyce's singing voice but was "scandalized" by his guitar playing.

Joyce in Zurich, December 1918.

33

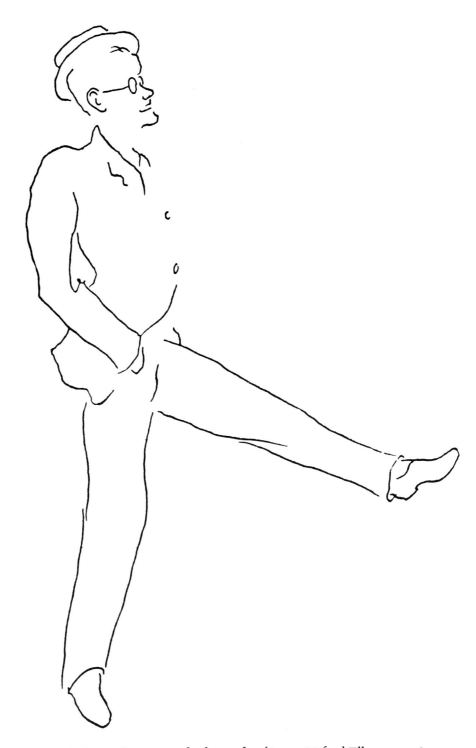

Desmond Harmsworth's sketch of Joyce dancing. In his biography of Joyce, Richard Ellmann wrote that "he might suddenly interrupt a Saturday afternoon walk in the fashionable Bahnhofstrasse [in Zurich] by flinging his loose limbs about in a kind of spider dance, the effect accentuated by his tight trouser-legs and wide cloak, diminutive hat, and thin cane."

James Joyce at age 41 during a holiday in Bognor, Sussex, in 1923. Joyce had just finished writing Ulysses and his wife, Nora, lamented to her sister Kathleen, "He's on another book again."

Joyce and Sylvia Beach outside her bookstore, Shakespeare and Company, in 1920. She became publisher of Ulysses after the U.S. Post Office confiscated and burned copies of a literary magazine that contained sections from it, frightening away U.S. and British publishers.

Joyce and Sylvia Beach
at Shakespeare
and Company, 1921.

Paul-Émile Bécat's drawing of Joyce and Robert McAlmon, an American poet and friend from the early 1920s in Paris.

Two photos by Man Ray, one of many noted photographers and
other artists who depicted Joyce beginning in the early 1920s.

By *his thirties, the publication of excerpts*
from Ulysses *was adding to the reputation Joyce had gained in*
literary circles as the author of Dubliners,
A Portrait of the Artist, *and* Exiles.

A David Levine drawing of Joyce, 1988.

A Perhaps he was a woman. *oohy Ophelia committ*
suicide. 48

Wonder is he pimping after me?

Mr Bloom stood at the corner, his eyes wandering over the multicoloure
hoardings. Cantrell and Cochrane's. Ginger Ale (Aromatic). Clery's summe
sale. No, he's going on straight. Hello. *Leah* tonight : Mrs Bandman Palme
Like to see her in that again. Hamlet she played last night. Male impersonato
Poor papa! How he used to talk about Kate Bateman in that! Outside th
Adelphi in London waited all the afternoon to get in. Year before I was bor
that was : sixtyfive. And Ristori in Vienna. What is this the right name is
By Mosenthal it is. Rachel, is it? No. The scene he was always talking abou
where the old blind Abraham recognises the voice and puts his fingers on hi
face.

— Nathan's voice! His son's voice! hear the voice of Nathan who lef
his father to die of grief and misery in my arms, who left the house of his
father and left the God of his father.

Every word is so deep, Leopold.

Poor papa! Poor man! I'm glad. I didn't go into the room to look at his
face. That day! O dear! O dear! Ffoo! Well, perhaps it was the best for him.

Mr Bloom went round the corner and passed the drooping ~~horses~~ of the
hazard. No use thinking of it any more. Nosebag time. Wish I hadn't met that
M'Coy fellow. He came nearer and heard a crunching of the oats, the gently
champing teeth. Their full buck eyes regarded him as he went by ⌄ Poor
jugginses! Damn all they know or care about anything with their long noses
stuck in nosebags. Too full for words. Still they get their feed all right and
their doss. Gelded too : a stump of black guttapercha wagging limp between
their haunches. Might be happy all the same that way. Good poor brutes they
look. F

He drew the letter from his pocket and folded it into the newspaper he
carried. Might just walk into her here. The lane is safer.

He ~~hummed~~, pass~~ing~~ the cabman's shelter. Curious the life of drifting
cabbies A

La ci darem la mano
La la lala la la.

He turned into Cumberland street and, going on some paces, halted in th e
lee of the station wall. No-one. Meade's timberyard. Piled balks. Ruins and
tenements. With careful tread he passed over a hopscotch court with its for-

⊢ nags

⌄ : amid the
sweet oaten
reek of ~~the~~
horsepiss.

F still their neigh
can be very
irritating.

⊓ ed

A all weathers, all places, time or
setdown, no will of their own. Voglio
e non. Like to give them an odd
cigarette. He hummed :

These pages from the fourth set of corrected proofs for the
1922 edition of Ulysses (published by Shakespeare and Company, Paris)
demonstrate how Joyce painstakingly reworked his fiction.

ten pickeystone. Not a sinner. Near the timberyard a squatted child at
rbles, alone, shooting the taw with a cunnythumb. Open it. When I played
rbles when went to that old dame's school. She liked mignonette. Mrs Ellis's.
d Mr? He opened the letter within the newspaper.

A flower. A yellow flower with flattened petals. Not annoyed then?
hat does she say?

I think it's a.

Dear Henry,

I got your last letter to me and thank you very much for it. I am sorry
u did not like my last letter. Why did you enclose the stamps? I am awfully
gry with you. I do wish I could punish you for that. I called you naughty
y because I do not like that other world. Please tell me what is the real
aning of that word. Are you not happy in your home you poor little naughty
y? I do wish I could do something for you. Please tell me what you think
poor me. I often think of the beautiful name you have. Dear Henry, when
ll we meet? I think of you so often you have no idea. I have never felt
yself so much drawn to a man as you. I feel so bad about. Please write me
ong letter and tell me more. Remember if you do not I will punish you. So
w you know what I will do to you, you naughty boy, if you do not wrote.
how I long to meet you. Henry dear, do not deny my request before my
tience are exhausted. Then I will tell you all. Goodbye now, naughty
rling. I have such a bad headache today and write soon to your longing

MARTHA.

P. S. Do tell me what kind of perfume does your wife use. I want to
ow.

cactus

A Angry tulips with you darling manflower punish your flian as if you don't please poor forgetmenot how I long violets to dear roses when we soon meet all naughty nightstalk wife Martha perfume. smelt its almost no smell smell

He tore the flower gravely from its pinhold and placed it in his heart
cket. Then, walking slowly forward, he read the letter again, murmuring
re and there a word. Having read it all he took it from the newspaper and
t it back in his sidepocket.

Weak joy opened his lips. Changed since the first letter. Doing the indi-

Language of flowers. They like it because no-one can hear. Or a poison bouquet to strike him down.

> "I've put in so many enigmas and puzzles that it will keep
> the professors busy for centuries arguing over what I meant,
> and that's the only way of insuring one's immortality."
> —Joyce, describing the writing of Ulysses

47

FROM LEFT: Ezra Pound, a leading advocate of Joyce's work, poses in his Paris studio in 1923 with attorney John Quinn, author Ford Madox Ford, and Joyce.

Photographs of Joyce and Lucia (LEFT) and Nora (RIGHT)
during a holiday in Ostend in 1924.

Berenice Abbott photographs of Joyce in 1929 and his
daughter Lucia in 1926. Joyce wrote, "Whatever spark of
gift I possess has been transmitted to Lucia,
and has kindled a fire in her brain."

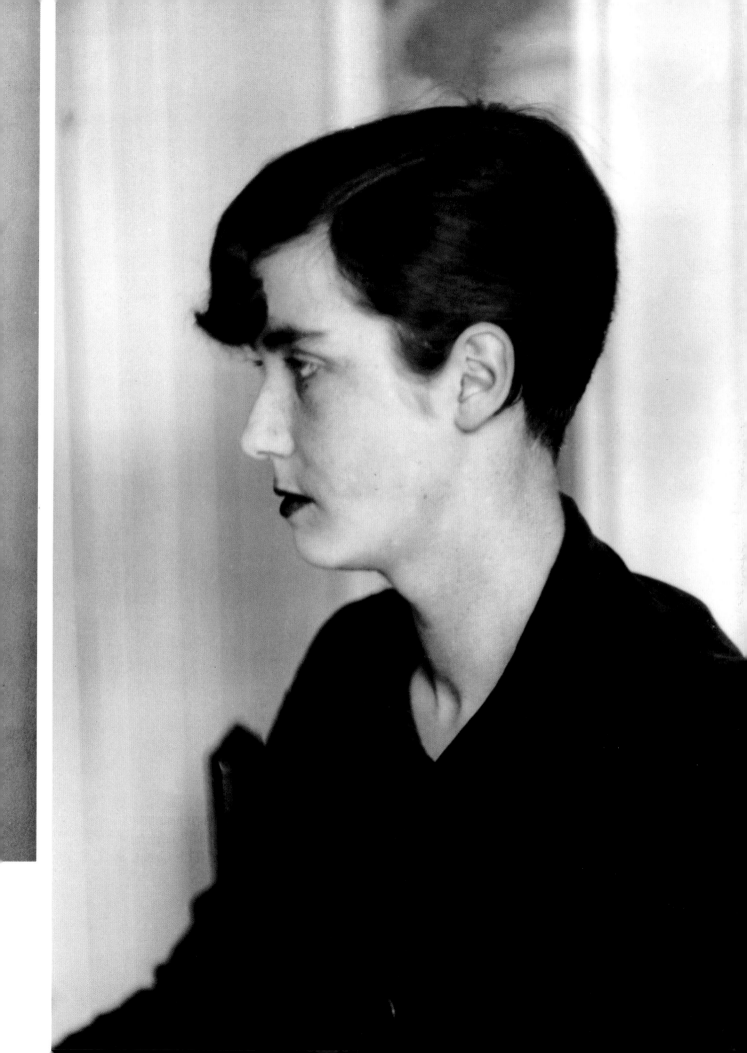

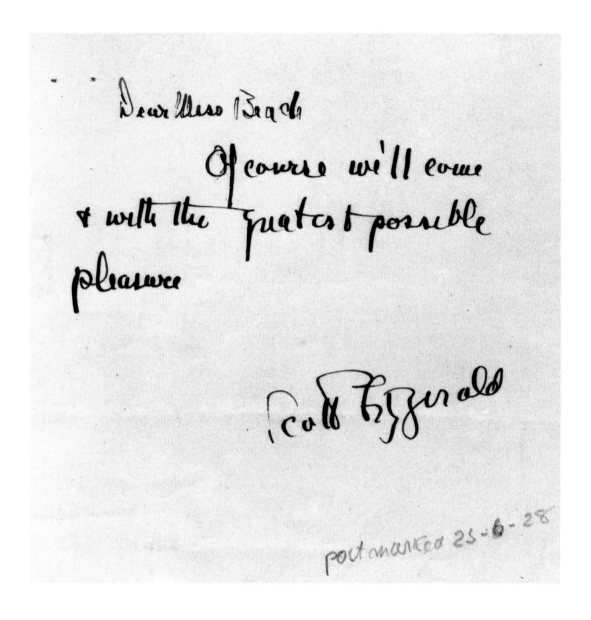

Dear Miss Beach

Of course we'll come
+ with the greatest possible
pleasure

Scott Fitzgerald

postmarked 25-6-28

F. Scott Fitzgerald's drawing of an evening at Adrienne Monnier's Paris apartment, in which he is kneeling to "St. James" Joyce, while Monnier and Sylvia Beach appear as mermaids. He sent the drawing to Beach on the flyleaf of his novel The Great Gatsby in 1928.

To celebrate the 25th anniversary of Bloomsday in June 1929, Adrienne Monnier hosted a Déjeuner "Ulysses" at the Hôtel Léopold in Les-Vaux-de-Cernay. Seated, from the left, were: Philippe Soupault, Nora Joyce, Edouard Dujardin, Paul Valéry, James Joyce, and Léon Paul Fargue. Behind them, from the left, were:

Jeanne Bouquet, Helen Joyce, Charles de la Morandière, Lucia Joyce, Lucienne Astrue, Philippe Fontaine, Thomas McGreevy, Léon Rivet, Marc Chadourne, Sylvia Beach, Adrienne Monnier, Jules Romains, Mrs. Paul Valéry, André Chamson, Marie Scheikévitch, and Pierre de Lapuy.

The Joyce family in Paris, 1924.

Man Ray's photograph of Giorgio and Helen Joyce
at the time of their wedding in 1930.

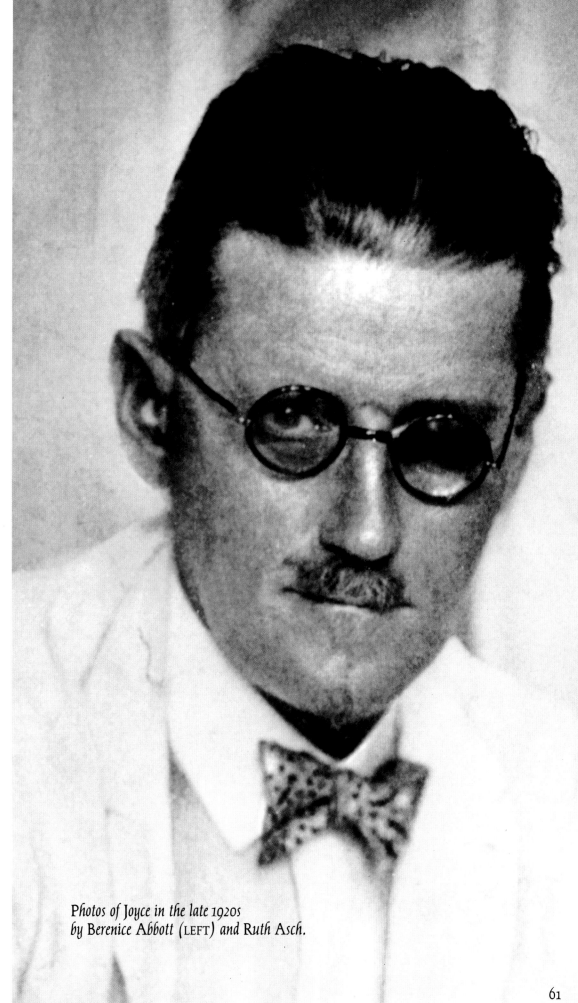

Photos of Joyce in the late 1920s
by Berenice Abbott (LEFT) and Ruth Asch.

Joyce, Nora, and Lucia on holiday, 1932.

*Joyce with (from left) Lucia, an unidentified woman,
his brother Stanislaus, and Stanislaus's wife,
Nelly, in Salzburg, 1928.*

James and Nora with Moune Gilbert at Torquay in 1929.

A portrait of Nora by Berenice Abbott.

On the beach at Scheveningen, Holland, in the late 1920s.

Joyce after one of his many eye operations, south of France, 1922.

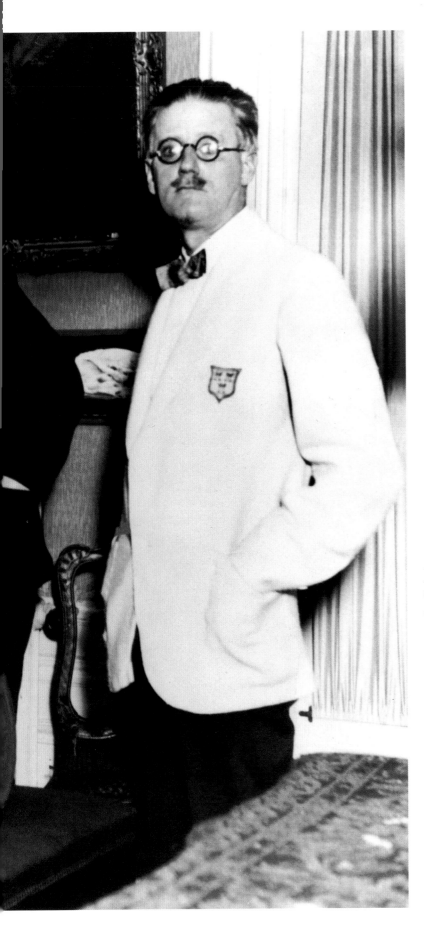

James and Nora with tenor John Sullivan
and his wife, about 1930,
at the time Joyce became a tireless
advocate of Sullivan's career.

Joyce said, "Paul Léon tells me that when I stand bent over at a street corner,
I look like a question mark." This anecdote inspired César Abin to draw Joyce
as a question mark for his 50th birthday portrait in transition magazine.

One of Augustus John's 1930 set of drawings of Joyce.

Brancusi's drawing of Joyce for publication of a section of Finnegans Wake.

Nora in 1932.
"Being married to a writer is a very hard life." NORA JOYCE

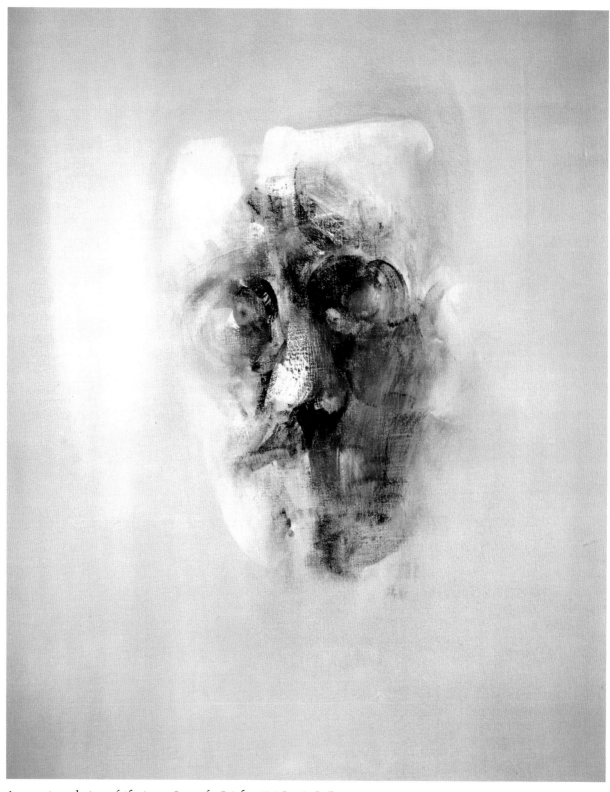

A recent rendering of the inner Joyce by Irish artist Louis LeBrocquy,
which appears in a catalog of LeBrocquy's work from 1975 to 1987.

A 1930 bust of Joyce by the sculptor Jo Davidson, who
four years earlier had arranged for a production of
Joyce's play Exiles in New York.

Joyce with Augustus John
in the artist's
Paris studio in 1930.

Two drawings of Joyce:
on the left, by his daughter, Lucia;
on the right, by Augustus John.

Joyce captioned this photograph of himself, author James Stephens (left), and tenor John Sullivan "Three Irish Beauties." Fearful about his failing eyesight, Joyce half-seriously asked Stephens to finish Finnegans Wake for him.

Almost 30 years after they met, James and Nora finally married in London in 1931, with their solicitor as witness and British paparazzi in full pursuit.

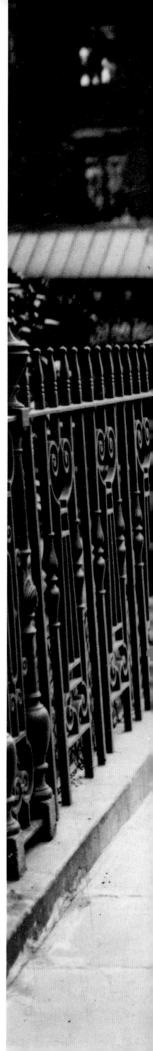

In 1932, the Joyces took their troubled daughter, Lucia, on vacation to Lake Constance, where they were photographed over lunch with an unidentified girl.

Lucia and Nora ride in the back of the car,
while Lucia's nurse sits next to Joyce during a trip
to Feldkirch, Switzerland, in 1932.

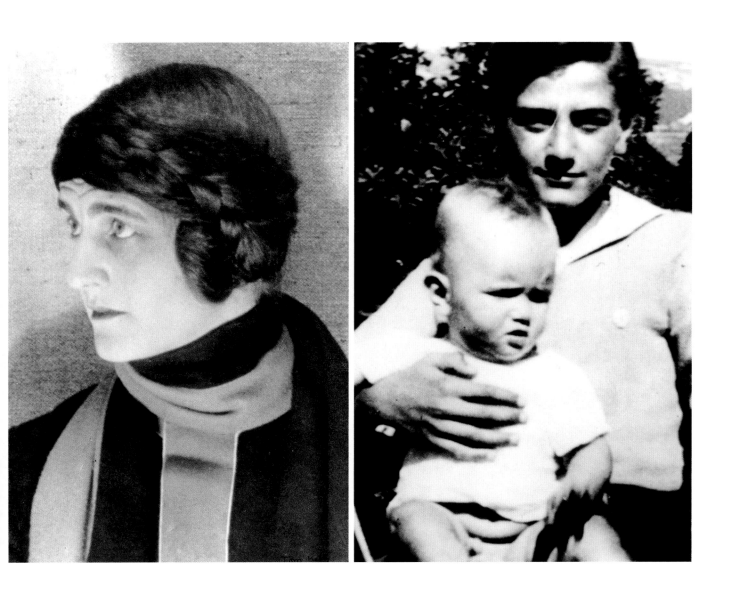

LEFT: *Helen Fleischman and Giorgio Joyce in the late 1920s.*
ABOVE: *Helen in the 1930s; her one-year-old son Stephen and his half-brother, David Fleischman.*

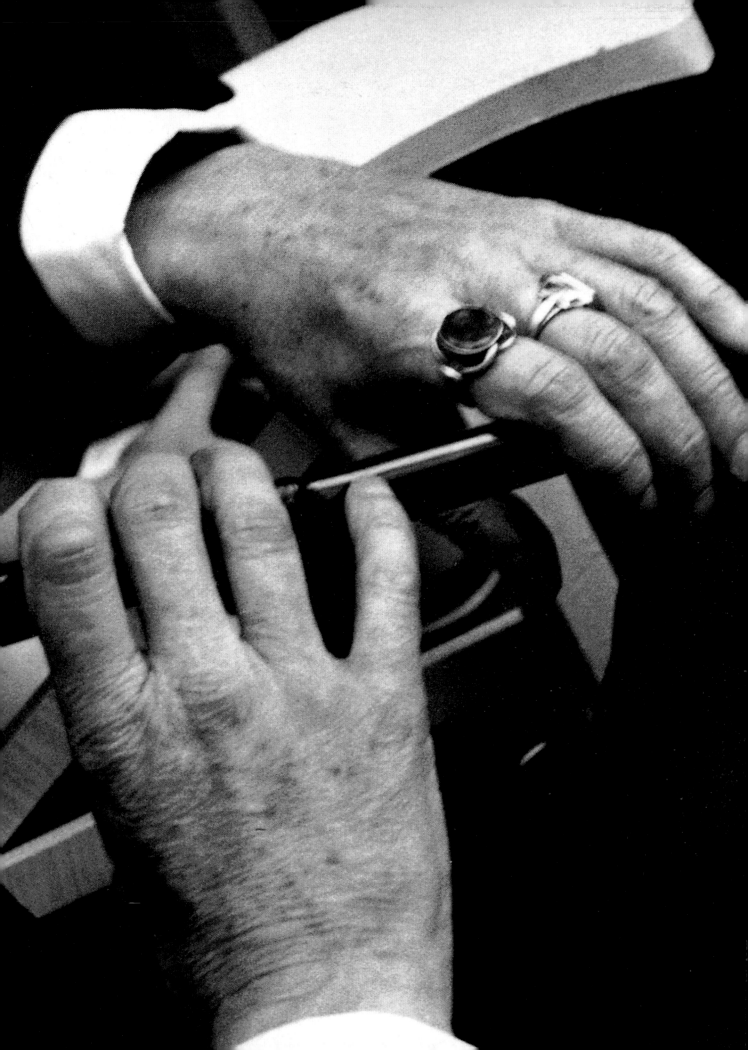

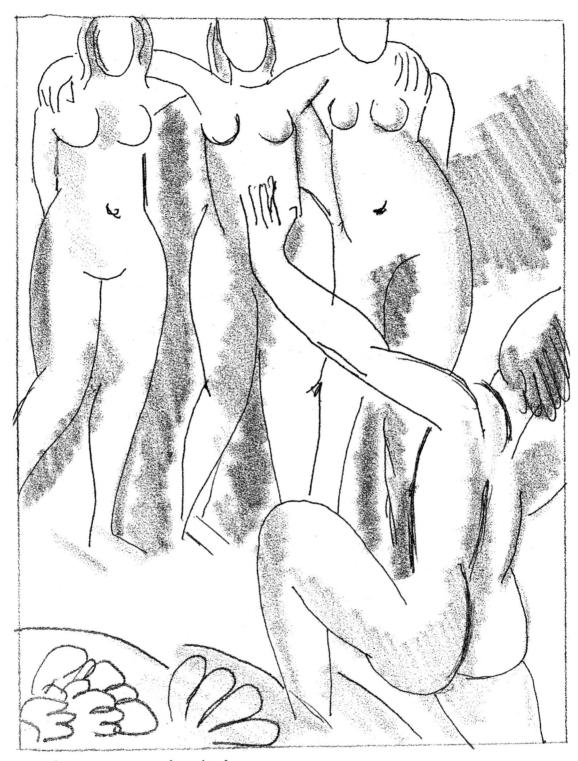

One of Henri Matisse's etchings for the 1935
publication of Ulysses by the Limited Editions Club in New York,
based not on Joyce's novel but on Homer's Odyssey.

Gisèle Freund, who photographed Joyce in 1938, noted
that he held his cane as if it were a musical instrument.

*The photos on these pages and overleaf
are from a sitting in the mid-1930s
with the French photographer Lipnitski.*

LEFT: *Joyce relaxing during a photo session with*
Gisèle Freund in 1938. ABOVE: *With fellow writer James Stephens.*

Gisèle Freund's photograph
of Joyce, Sylvia Beach,
and Adrienne Monnier,
taken at Shakespeare
and Company in 1938 prior
to the publication
of Finnegans Wake.

Gisèle Freund's photographs of Joyce at the piano and with his son, Giorgio, and
grandson, Stephen, beneath Patrick Tuohy's portrait of James's father, John.
"My grandfather attached special importance to this photograph,
consistent with his feelings about his family," says Stephen.

*Two photographs of Joyce from the late 1930s.
On the left, he is in Lucerne with Nora,
Hans Curjel, and Carola Giedion-Welcker.*

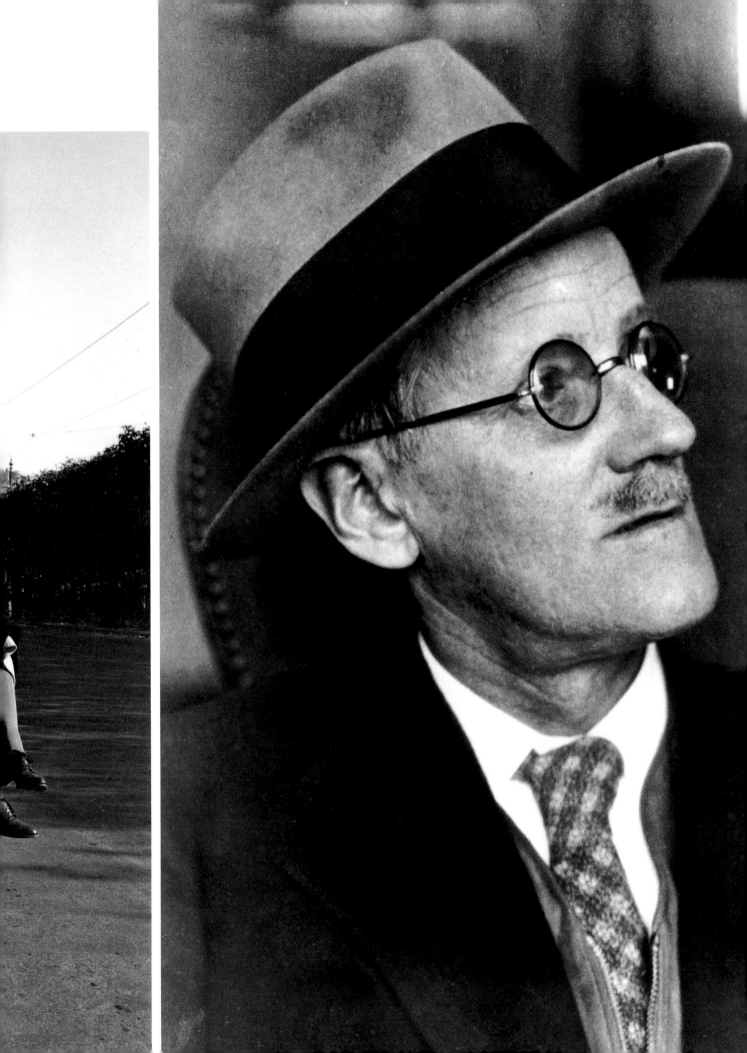

Joyce's friend Carola Giedion-Welcker photographed him
at the Platzspitz in Zurich in 1938. Stephen Joyce describes
these pictures as "the most characteristic photographs
of my grandfather and my two favorites."